God is Wise

God is Wise

A children's book produced by
The Bible Tells Me So Press

Copyright © 2019
The Bible Tells Me So Corporation

All rights reserved. No part of this book, neither text nor illustrations, may be reproduced without permission in writing by the publisher.

PUBLISHED BY
THE BIBLE TELLS ME SO CORPORATION
WWW.THEBIBLETELLSMESO.COM

First Printing July, 2019

When we view the earth

and how it was made,

The clouds that float by,

thick, puffy, and round,

that
falls
to
the
ground.

The dandelion

has seeds
    that take flight;

the wind takes them to

good
soil
and
light.

Our God, He is wise.

and knows what we need.

God's wisdom is seen
in all that we view,

but mostly
it's seen...

in how He made you.

Jehovah by wisdom
founded the earth;
He established the heavens
by understanding;

Proverbs 3:19

For more
books, videos, songs, and crafts,
visit us online at
TheBibleTellsMeSo.com

Standing on the Bible and growing!